THE
TESTING
OF YOUR
FAITH

Dr. Bruce H. Wilkinson

A Walk Thru the Bible Classic

The Testing of Your Faith Workbook

Designer: Michelle Strickland

Published by Walk Thru the Bible Ministries
4201 North Peachtree Road, Atlanta, Georgia 30341-1207
www.walkthru.org   1-800-361-6131

THE
TESTING
OF YOUR
FAITH

Contents

TAKE A WALK. CHANGE THE WORLD.

*Helping people everywhere live God's Word ...
and love God's Word.*

That's where "igniting a passion," a phrase we use frequently, comes in. Our mission is to create a path to help people encounter God, to connect them with His heart and open their ears to His voice. We believe that making disciples is more than simply making converts; it's helping people cultivate a dynamic, growing relationship with God. And igniting a passion for His Word is a vital part of that mission.

How do we do that?

By getting people into His Word every way we know how, and with an approach that's engaging, relevant, and memorable—even exciting and fun! In our live events, we race through the Old or New Testament in a few hours. With our devotionals, we linger in the Bible over the course of a year. With our small group resources, we walk through the Bible—actually portions of it or topics from it—in a few weeks. We partner with local churches around the world to provide teaching, tools, and training to pastors, leaders, and all other believers with solid, biblical resources. And over the course of three decades, our discipleship materials have reached millions of people. Walk Thru the Bible ignites a passion for God's Word through innovative live events, inspiring biblical resources, and a global impact that changes lives world-wide . . . including yours.

Step into the Story: Innovative Live Events

Experience live events that unveil God's Word as you've never known it before. Our live events tell God's story in a way that's interactive, relevant, and fun. As you're learning God's story, you're developing insight into yours—and enjoying an adventure that will last a lifetime. We offer more than 10 different live events, including: *Walk Thru the Old Testament* (for adults) *OT Live* (for students) *Kids in the Book* (for children)

Take a Walk: Biblical Resources

Delve into resources that impact your spiritual journey wherever you are. For more than three decades, we have developed resources that help people grow in their relationship with God and apply His Word to daily life. We do that through Bibles, small group studies, devotional magazines, books, and more.

Suggested resources after experiencing *The Testing of Your Faith:*

Walk Thru the Bible Small Group Discussion Guides
Story Thru the Bible (52 Bible Stories with discussion questions)
Raise Up a Child DVD Study
A Biblical Portrait of a Marriage DVD Study

Change the World: Global Impact

Get involved in a global ministry that impacts lives around the world. Walk Thru the Bible is dedicated to developing a global network of pastors and Christian leaders who make life-changing biblical resources available worldwide. Our global network has helped to change lives, preserve families, address social needs, and inspire churches in more than 100 countries. Reaching their communities in dramatic ways, our global partners are helping to change the world, one person at a time, through the power of God's Word.

Visit us at www.walkthru.org

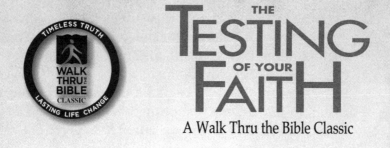

THE TESTING OF YOUR FAITH

A Walk Thru the Bible Classic

A Word from Walk Thru the Bible

The Testing of Your Faith is one of our Classic Series DVD studies. Our Classics are those studies that have provided such rich spiritual awareness and deep personal growth that they have remained relevant over the course of time.

The Testing of Your Faith was filmed in 1997, and since then, the series has changed the way thousands of believers understand and live their faith. The material is just as relevant and timely today as when the series was first introduced by Bruce Wilkinson, founder of Walk Thru the Bible.

Through *The Testing of Your Faith* you'll discover transformational truths about why we are tested, how we are to live while being tested, and how to trust God during our trials. You'll learn how every Christian can build his or her faith during tests, receive the key to successfully passing a test of your faith, and how to have peace while in the midst of a storm. And you'll come away filled with a fresh confidence and trust in God's plan for your life.

We are honored to bring you this study and pray you are blessed by your journey.

Walk Thru the Bible • www.walkthru.org • 1-800-361-6131

THE
TESTING
OF YOUR
FAITH

Passing the Test of Faith (Part One)

"My brethren, count it all joy
when you fall into various trials."
James 1:2-4

SESSION ONE

James 1:2-4
"My brethren, count it all joy when you fall into various trials, knowing that the testing of your faith produces patience. But let patience have its perfect work, that you may be perfect and complete, lacking nothing."

God's Goal

That we may become _____ , _____ , *and* _____ *nothing.*

Beliefs About The Test of Faith

1. God tests _____ believer many times in many different ways.

1 Peter 1:6-7 — "In this you greatly rejoice, though now for a little while, if need be, you have been grieved by various trials, that the genuineness of your faith, being much more precious than gold that perishes, though it is tested by fire, may be found to the praise, honor, and glory at the revelation of Jesus Christ."

7 Principles of the Test of Faith

- The test is only for a _____.
- If _____ be.
- Every test brings _____ of some kind.
- There are _____ trials.
- God brings the trials so that we have _____ of faith.
- Our faith is more _____ than gold.
- Your _____ is God's glory at the second coming.

2. God knows _____ about your tests.

Read Matthew 11:2-5

Matthew 11:6—"And blessed is he who is not offended because of Me."

3. God is with you in _____ tests.

Read Daniel 3:15-16, Daniel 3:25

Daniel 3:17-18—"If that is the case, our God whom we serve is able to deliver us from the burning fiery furnace, and He will deliver us from your hand, O king. But if not, let it be known to you, O king, that we do not serve your gods, nor do we worship the gold image which you have set up."

4. God is ultimately in _____ all the time.

The test of Job — Read Job 1:13-19

Job 1:20-21—"Then Job arose and tore his robe and shaved his head, and he fell to the ground and worshipped. And he said: 'Naked I came from my mother's womb and naked shall I return there. The LORD gave, and the LORD has taken away; Blessed be the name of the Lord.' "

5. God has _____ power.

Read Numbers 11:10, 13, 18-20, 22, 31-32

Numbers 11:23—And the LORD said to Moses, "Has the LORD's arm been shortened? No shall see whether My word will befall you or not."

Group Discussion

Take a few moments to consider these questions, then discuss.

What do you consider to be the purpose of the test of faith?

_____

_____

_____

What test of faith have you failed? What test have you passed?

_____

_____

_____

On a Personal Level

	Never	Occasionally	Often
I experience that God is testing my faith.	O	O	O
I am focused on passing the test of faith.	O	O	O
I am patient when God tests my faith.	O	O	O
My knowledge of God helps me to endure my test of faith.	O	O	O
Tests of faith help me to grow spiritually.	O	O	O

Self Assessment

Is your belief about tests of faith lacking, growing or good?

THE
TESTING
OF YOUR
FAITH

Passing the Test of Faith (Part Two)

"And we know that all things work together for the good of those who love God." Romans 8:28

SESSION TWO

The test of faith is designed for our own good, and it is exactly what God has planned for us.

The Test Consists of

- What do I believe about God?

- How much do I believe that the test is from God?

_____

_____

_____

Beliefs About The Test of Faith

6. God expects you to _____ the test.

- God wants us to believe more and more in Him. Therefore He expects us to pass the test.

- When the tests comes it is always about God and what we believe about Him. It is never about what we believe about ourselves. That's why the test is always greater than we are.

Read Genesis 22:1-2, 16-17

Genesis 22:8, 12—And Abraham said, "My son, God will provide for Himself the lamb for a burnt offering." And He said, "Do not lay your hand on the lad, or do anything to him; for now I know that you fear God, since you have not withheld your son, your only son, from Me."

7. God has your ultimate _____ as His purpose.

• This test is designed for you, and only you.

• If there was a better way, God would have taken it.

• Nothing comes to you that God doesn't know about and that is not under His ultimate control. There is NO exception.

Genesis 50:19-20—Joseph said to them, "Do not be afraid, for I am in the place of God: But as for you, you meant evil against me; but God *meant* it for good, in order to bring it about as it is this day, to save many people alive."

Romans 8:28—"And we know that *all* things work together for good."

What will be able to separate you from God's love?

Romans 8:35—"Who shall separate us from the love of Christ? Shall tribulation, or distress, or persecution, or famine, or nakedness, or peril, or sword?"

Romans 8:37-39—"Yet in all things we are more than conquerors through Him who loved us. For I am persuaded that neither death nor life, nor angels nor principalities, nor powers, nor things present nor things to come, nor height nor depth, nor any other created thing, shall be able to separate us from the love of God which is in Jesus Christ our LORD."

Group Discussion

Take a few moments to consider these questions, then discuss.

What did you learn during the session? _____

_____

When people say God is not fair or He is uninvolved, how do we respond? _____

_____

What test might be too difficult for you to pass at present?

_____

_____

On a Personal Level

When did you start believing in Jesus Christ as your Lord and Savior? _____

_____

Do you really believe God is in control? _____

_____

Which victory of faith do you consider to be your greatest?

_____

_____

Is there any bitterness or unbelief in you at present toward God? _____

_____

THE
TESTING
OF YOUR
FAITH

Wrong Responses to the Test of Faith

"And you shall remember that the LORD your
God led you all the way these forty years in
the wilderness, to humble you and test you,
to know what was in your heart, whether you
would keep His Commandments or not."
Deuteronomy 8:2

SESSION THREE

Wrong Responses

• If you are obedient to God you are _____

• If you are disobedient to God you are _____

Deuteronomy 8:1-3 — "Every commandment which I command you today you must be careful to observe, that you may live and multiply, and go in and possess the land of which the LORD swore to your fathers. And you shall remember that the LORD your God led you all the way these forty years in the wilderness, to *humble you* and *test you,* to know what was in your heart, whether you would keep His Commandments or not. So He humbled you, *allowed* you to hunger, and fed you with manna which you did not know nor did your fathers know, that He might make you know that man shall not live by bread alone; but man lives by every word that proceeds from the mouth of the LORD."

Read Deuteronomy 8:16 . . . to do good in the end!

1. The Test—Exodus 15:22-23

• Did God know the water was bitter?
• Could God have made it sweet before they got there?

Exodus 15:24-25 — "And the people *murmured* against Moses saying 'What shall we drink?' So he cried out to the LORD, and the LORD showed him a tree; and when he cast it into the water, the waters were made sweet. There he made a statute and an ordinance for them. And there He tested them."

2. The Test—Exodus 16:1

Exodus 16:2—"Then the whole congregation of the children of Israel *murmured against Moses and Aaron* in the wilderness."

Read Exodus 16:3-4, 13

3. The Test—Exodus 17:1,3,7

Exodus 17:2—"Therefore the people contended with Moses, and said, 'Give us water, that we may drink.' And Moses said to them, 'Why do you contend with me? Why do you *tempt the* LORD?' "

4. The Test—Numbers 11:1,4,5,19

Numbers 11:10—"Now Moses heard the *people weeping* throughout their families, everyone at the door of his tent; and the anger of the LORD was greatly aroused."

5. The Test—Numbers 13:32-33;14:2,8-10

Numbers 14:3—"Why has the LORD brought us to this land to fall by the sword, that our wives and children should become victims? Would it not be better to return to Egypt?" *So they said to one another,* "Let us select a leader and return to Egypt."

Five Wrong Responses

1. We _____ our faith.
2. We _____ about the circumstances.
3. We _____ the people in charge.
4. We come _____ the LORD in _____.
5. We will _____ other people's _____.

Group Discussion

Take a few moments to consider these questions, then discuss.

Give a short summary on why people fail their test of faith.

_____

_____

When listening to the average churchgoer's discussions on church leaders or politicians, do they fail or pass the test?

_____

Why do believers complain about their circumstances?

_____

_____

On a Personal Level

	Never	Occasionally	Often
I compromise my faith.	○	○	○
I complain about my circumstances.	○	○	○
I criticize the people in charge.	○	○	○
I come against the Lord in anger.	○	○	○
I corrupt other people's faith.	○	○	○
When tested do you sometimes project contentment, but secretly you are rebellious in your heart toward God?	○	○	○

Self Assessment

Is your response to tests of faith lacking, growing or good?

THE
TESTING
OF YOUR
FAITH

Right Responses to the Test of Faith

"But My servant Caleb, because he has a
different spirit in him and has followed Me
fully, I will bring into the land where he went,
and his descendants shall inherit it."
Numbers 14:24

SESSION FOUR

Most of the time we fail the test of faith because we don't know what the Bible teaches.

Right Beliefs About God

1. God _____ teaches you before testing you.

- Everything that precedes the test of faith is an overwhelming teaching by God that you can trust God for

_____.

- We can trust God because His history is flawless.

Exodus 14:30-31—"So the Lord saved Israel that day out of the hand of the Egyptians, and Israel saw the Egyptians dead on the seashore. Thus Israel saw the great work which the Lord had done in Egypt; so the people feared the Lord, and believed the Lord and his servant Moses."

- We believe the past about God's trustworthy character.
- It is not the amount of faith we have in God—it is how much we believe that God is faithful that enables us to believe.

The Covenant God made with His People

Between the tests in Exodus and the tests in Numbers God made a _____ with Israel.

Exodus 19:4-6—"You have seen what I did to the Egyptians, and how I bore you on eagle's wings and brought you to Myself. Now therefore, if you will indeed obey My voice and keep my covenant, then you shall be a special treasure to Me above all people; for all the earth is Mine. And you shall be to Me a kingdom of priests and a holy nation."

Israel's answer: Exodus 24:3

2. God always takes our _____ personally.

• If we _____ and _____ we do it against God and not against the people around us. God takes it personally.

Exodus 17:2, 7—"Therefore the people contended with Moses, and said 'Give us water, that we may drink.' And Moses said to them, 'Why do you contend with me? Why do you *tempt the LORD?'* So he called the name of the place Massah and Meribah because of the contention of the children of Israel, and because they *tempted the LORD, saying,* 'Is the LORD among us or not?' "

Read Psalm 78

3. God always _____ those who will rebel against Him in a test. God will always _____ those who believe in Him in the test.

• What happens when you rebel against God?

Read Numbers 14:22-23

Numbers 14:27-29—"How long shall I bear this evil congregation who murmur against Me? I have heard the murmurings which the children of Israel murmur against Me. Saying to them, 'As I live,' says the LORD. 'just as you have spoken in My hearing, so I will do to you: The carcasses of you who have murmured against Me shall fall in this wilderness.' "

• What happens when you believe in God?

Numbers 14:24—"But My servant Caleb, because he has a different spirit in him and has followed Me fully, I will bring into the land where he went, and his descendants shall inherit it."

Group Discussion

Take a few moments to consider these questions, then discuss.

What have you learned about the right beliefs of the test of faith? _____

_____

_____

What is the consequence of either rebellion or obedience toward God? _____

_____

On a Personal Level

How did God prepare you for your most recent test?

_____

_____

Are there still aspects of your life that you murmur about?

_____

_____

When did you put your full trust in God? _____

_____

How did God bless you when you passed your last test of faith? _____

_____

THE
TESTING
OF YOUR
FAITH

The Anatomy of a Test of Faith (Part One)

"The Lord gives faith for the very purpose
of trying it for the glory of His own name,
and for the good of him who has it . . ."
George Mueller

SESSION FIVE

"The Lord gives faith for the very purpose of trying it for the glory of His own name, and for the good of him who has it; . . . and, by the very trial of our faith, we not only obtain blessing to our own souls, by becoming better acquainted with God, if we hold fast our confidence in Him, but our faith is also, by the exercise, strengthened: and so it comes, that, if we walk with God . . . the trails of faith will be greater and greater."—George Mueller

James 1:2-4—"My brethren, count it all joy when you fall into various trials, knowing that the testing of your faith produces patience. But let patience have its perfect work, that you may be perfect and complete, lacking nothing."

• The ultimate goal is to glorify God, and as a person to become mature, complete, and lacking in nothing.

How Do I Know I am in a Test of Faith?

1. I will feel _____ and distress.

1 Peter 1:6-7—"In this you greatly rejoice, though now for a little while, if need be, you have been grieved by various trials, that the genuineness of your faith, being much more precious than gold that perishes, though it is tested by fire, may be found to praise, honor, and glory at the revelation of Jesus Christ."

2. Feelings of impatience, anger or irritation are sometimes the result of being in a test of faith.

• We respond _____ to the situation.

3. The way you feel will influence the way you _____ .

4. Find out what _____ God is testing.

5. Change the _____ belief. Don't believe
a lie!

• If I change what I believe about a certain situation, it will
change my feelings and reaction.

When I am in a test of faith

• I am in a test from God.
• I respond emotionally.
• I act the emotion.
• I need to find out what belief God is testing.
• I need to change what I believe. The truth will set me free.

Philippians 4:11-13—"Not that I speak in regard to need, for
I have learned in whatever state I am, to be content: I know
how to be abased, and I know how to abound. Everywhere
and in all things I have learned both to abound and to suffer
need. I can do all things through Christ who strengthens me."

Work on what you believe and your behavior will follow.

Group Discussion

Take a few moments to consider these questions, then discuss.

What would you consider the essence of knowing that you are in a test of faith? _____

_____

Tell the group about a situation that you have solved and where you know that neither the person nor the situation changed, only your perceptions (beliefs).

On a Personal Level

Practical Analysis of Your Most Recent Test

• Describe the situation of your most recent test: _____

_____

• Describe your reactions:
  Emotions: _____

  Behaviors: _____

Remember: Changing your belief will change your emotions and behavior.

Which of your beliefs were tested? _____

What does the Bible say? _____

What lie should be substituted with the truth? _____

If you do not change your belief, will the test go away? ____

What behavior will be changed by believing the truth? ____

_____

THE
TESTING
OF YOUR
FAITH

The Anatomy of a Test of Faith (Part Two)

"For God has not given us a spirit of fear, but
of power and love and of a sound mind."
2 Timothy 1:7

SESSION SIX

How Not to Respond to the Test of Faith

Read Numbers 13:31-33

Numbers 14:1-4—"Then all the congregation lifted up their voices and cried, and the people wept that night. And all the children of Israel murmured against Moses and Aaron, and the whole congregation said to them, "If only we had died in the land of Egypt! Or if only we had died in this wilderness! Why has the LORD brought us to this land to fall by the sword, that our wives and children should become victims? Would it not be better to return to Egypt? So they said to one another, "Let us select a leader and return to Egypt."

How to Respond to the Test of Faith

Numbers 14:8-10—"If the LORD delights in us, then He will bring us into this land and give it to us, 'a land which flows with milk and honey.' Only do not rebel against the LORD nor fear the people of the land, for they are our bread; their protection has departed from them, and the LORD is with us. Do not fear them. And all the congregation said to stone him with stones."

- 10 of the spies responded in fear.
- 2 of the spies responded in faith.

The fear comes from looking at the people and the circumstances and taking your eyes off the Lord. The outcome of every test of faith depends on how I look at the test.

1 Samuel 17:24—"And all the men of Israel, when they saw the man, fled from him and were dreadfully afraid."

- The opposite of fear is _____ in what I believe.

Read 1 Samuel 17:31-34

- David looked back at the _____ to strengthen his faith.

1 Samuel 17:35-36 — "I went out after it and struck it, and delivered the lamb from its mouth; and when it arose against me, I caught it by its beard, and struck it and killed it. Your servant has killed both lion and bear; and this uncircumcised Philistine will be like one of them, seeing he has defied the armies of the living God."

• The test of faith is not what you believe about yourself, but what you believe about the Lord.

Read 1 Samuel 17:37,44

1 Samuel 17:45 — "Then David said to the Philistine, "You come to me with a sword and a spear, and with javelin. But I come to you in the name of the LORD of hosts, the God of the armies of Israel, whom you have defied."

• The Lord's tests are always greater than we are.

Read 1 Samuel 17:46

• The test is for God's _____ and my good.

1 Samuel 17:46-47 — " . . . that all the earth may know that there is a God in Israel. Then all the assembly shall know that the LORD does not save with sword and spear; for the battle is the LORD's and He will give you into our hands."

The Test of the Disciples — Matthew 8:23-26

Should we be afraid? NO!

2 Timothy 1:7 — "For God has not given us a spirit of fear, but of power and love and of a sound mind."

What does a person with no fear look like?

Read Acts 20:22-24

Group Discussion

Take a few moments to consider these questions, then discuss.

What do you regard as the most important truth of this session?

_____

_____

Share with the group a test where God showed you He can overcome everything. _____

You may wish to share with the group about your "Goliath" that still seems insurmountable. _____

_____

On a Personal Level

	Never	Occasionally	Often
How frequently do you experience fear?	O	O	O
How frequently are you proud and arrogant?	O	O	O
How frequently do you use your own resources to conquer your fears?	O	O	O
How frequently do you forget that nothing is too big for God to handle?	O	O	O
How frequently do you experience a situation as hopeless?	O	O	O

Self Assessment
Are you passing these tests well?

THE
TESTING
OF YOUR
FAITH

When Faith Begins to Fail

"That they may set their hope in God,
and not forget the works of God,
but keep His commandments."
Psalm 78:7

What Should You Do When You Start to Lose Faith? _____

_____

_____

How do I strengthen my faith?

Psalm 78:7,8,10,11—"That they may set their hope in God, and not forget the works of God, but keep His commandments; And may not be like their fathers, a stubborn and rebellious generation, a generation that did not set its heart aright, and whose spirit was not faithful to God. They did not keep the covenant of God; they refused to walk in his law, 11and forgot His works and His wonders He had shown them."

We Should Do Three Things
- Set your _____ in God.
- Don't _____ the works of God.
- Keep His _____ .

When our faith starts to weaken, we should look at the Past, Present, and Future to restore our faith.

- The Past
The _____ we have about God coming through during a test.

- The Future
The _____ God has given to all of us.

- The Present
Stand on the _____ and _____ we have.

You use your faith in the Present. To restore your faith you look at the Past and the Future.

• Determination comes from faith and does not cause faith.

• The people who please God are the people who live by
_____ .

The Past, Present, and Future of the Old Testament

Past—The first _____ books of the Old Testament.
Future—The last _____ books of the Old Testament.
Present—All of the books in the middle (5).

The Past, Present, and Future of the New Testament

Past—Matthew, Mark, Luke, John, Acts.
Future—Revelation.
Present—All of the books in the middle.

• If we fail the test we start to believe a lie.
• People who don't pass the test of faith are called rebellious.

Read Psalm 78:7,8,11

Psalm 78:22,32,40,42—"Because they did not believe in God, and did not trust in His salvation. In spite of this they still sinned, and did not believe His wondrous works. How often they provoked Him in the desert! Yes, again and again they tempted God, and limited the Holy One of Israel. They did not remember His power."

The Secret of the Test of Faith
You need to remember what God has done for you in the past.

Group Discussion

Take a few moments to consider these questions, then discuss.

Summarize what you should do if your faith begins to fail.

_____

_____

_____

Discuss how God's children's rebellion against Him often has to do with their hopes and memories. _____

_____

_____

On a Personal Level

	Never	Occasionally	Often
How often don't you trust God?	O	O	O
How often do you feel there's no hope?	O	O	O
How often do you grieve God?	O	O	O
How often do you forget God's faithfulness in the past?	O	O	O
How often are you rebellious against God?	O	O	O

Self Assessment

Is your faith during tests and trials growing since beginning this study?

THE
TESTING
OF YOUR
FAITH

How to Remember Never to Forget

"So then faith comes by hearing
and hearing by the Word of God."
Romans 10:17

SESSION EIGHT

How to Remember

1. We must read the Bible _____ .

Romans 10:17—"So then faith comes by hearing and hearing by the word of God."

• The best place to learn about God is in the Bible.

2. _____ in your personal journal.

• If we don't record our life with Him, we will never become mighty in faith and obedient before Him.

3. Repeat _____ recent works of God and give thanks.

4. _____ the lives of the greats of the faith.

• Copy what the greats did in their tests of faith.

5. Retain the the victory in the test with _____ .

What is a Memorial?

It is something you build or keep to remember. It is a tangible object.

Joshua 4:6,7—"This may be a sign among you when your children ask in time to come, saying, 'What do these stones mean to you?' Then you shall answer them that the waters of the Jordan were cut off before the ark of the covenant of the LORD; when it crossed over the Jordan, the waters of the Jordan were cut off. And these stones shall be for a memorial to the children of Israel forever."

• It can be a memorial with good or bad memories.

6. Reconsider the Lord's faithfulness through the songs of faith.

7. Rehearse the test of faith with your family.

• Describe your experiences of a test of faith that you will share with your family. _____

_____

_____

_____

_____

_____

_____

Group Discussion

Take a few moments to consider these questions, then discuss.

What will you do to remember never to forget?

_____

_____

Share with the group events in your life where God showed His faithfulness. _____

_____

Share with the group a book you have read about a spiritual leader's journey of faith. _____

_____

On a Personal Level

Make a list of the things you can be thankful for.

_____

_____

Which spiritual experience can you share with your children? _____

_____

_____

_____

THE
TESTING
OF YOUR
FAITH

Holding on to Hope

"This hope we have as an anchor of the soul,
both sure and steadfast."
Hebrews 6:19

SESSION NINE

God Gives Us Hope

- We can claim all the promises that start with "Whosoever" and "Any one who desires."

- There are more than 30,000 promises in the Bible.

- God will keep every promise He makes.

All the failures of the test of faith have to do with what we believe about the future.

Hebrews 6:11,12—"And we desire that each one of you show the same diligence to the full assurance of hope until the end, that you do not become sluggish, but imitate those who through faith and patience inherit the promises."

- When you want to give in, look at someone who has passed the test and imitate him.

Hebrews 6:13,14—"For when God made a promise to Abraham, because He could swear by no one greater, He swore by Himself, saying, 'Surely blessing I will bless you, and multiplying I will multiply you.'

"And so, after he had patiently endured, he obtained the promise. For men indeed swear by the greater, and an oath for confirmation is for them an end of all dispute."

Hebrews 6:17,18—"Thus God, determining to show more abundantly to the heirs of promise the immutability of His counsel, confirmed it by an oath, that by two immutable things, in which it is impossible for God to lie, we might have strong consolation, who have fled for refuge to lay hold of the hope set before us."

• We can trust God that His promises will be fulfilled.

• When we are in a test and we want to run away we should look to the future and find a promise to strengthen our faith.

Hebrews 6:19,20—"This hope we have as an anchor of the soul, both sure and steadfast, and which enters the Presence behind the veil, where the forerunner has entered for us, even Jesus, having become High Priest forever according to the order of Melchizedek."

• Hope is the anchor of our souls.

• Behind the veil is the very Presence of God.

• The anchor goes through to the forerunner, Jesus.

Read Hebrews 10:36;11:8,9,11

The links of all the tests of faith are based upon whether or not you believe what God has promised.

Group Discussion

Take a few moments to consider these questions, then discuss.

Why is hope so important? _____

_____

_____

Share with the person next to you a promise that gave you hope. _____

_____

_____

On a Personal Level

	Never	Occasionally	Often
How often do you reflect on God's 30,000 promises?	O	O	O
How often do you claim the promises?	O	O	O
Do you always believe the promises in the Bible?	O	O	O
Do you keep on trusting even in the face of adversity?	O	O	O
How many times is your hope in God your only anchor?	O	O	O

Self Assessment

Are you holding on to hope or wavering?

THE
TESTING
OF YOUR
FAITH

Claiming the Promises

"Be anxious for nothing, but in everything
by prayer and supplication, with thanksgiving,
let your requests be made known to God."
Philippians 4:6

SESSION TEN

The Promise to Claim During Persecution

Matthew 5:11,12—"Blessed are you who when they revile and persecute you, and say all kinds of evil against you falsely for My sake. Rejoice and be exceedingly glad, for great is your reward in heaven, for so they persecuted the prophets who were before you."

When we are persecuted we have to do the following:
• We have to rejoice and be exceedingly happy.

The Promise:
• We will receive a great _____ in heaven.

The Promise to Claim When You Are Anxious

Philippians 4:6,7—"Be anxious for nothing, but in everything by prayer and supplication, with thanksgiving, let your requests be made known to God; and the peace of God, which surpasses all understanding, will guard your hearts and minds through Christ Jesus."

When we are anxious we have to do the following:
• Pray
• Give thanks to the Lord
• Let our _____ be known to God

The Promise:
• God will give you _____ that passes all understanding.

Read Matthew 6:25-30

Matthew 6:31-33—"Therefore do not worry, saying, 'What shall we eat?' or 'What shall we drink?' or 'What shall we wear?' For after all these things the Gentiles seek. For your heavenly Father knows that you need all these things. But seek first the kingdom of God and His righteousness, and all these things shall be added to you."

When we worry we have to do the following:
- _____ sin.
- _____ God.
- Rest.

The Promise:
- All the things will be added unto us.

The Promise to Claim When You Are Afraid

Hebrews 13:5,6—"Let your conduct be without covetousness; be content with such things as you have. For He Himself has said "I will never leave you or forsake you." So we may boldly say: "The LORD is my helper; I will not fear. What can man do to me?"

- Covetousness is always linked to _____ .

Read Joshua 1:5, 6, 7, 9

When we are afraid we have to do the following:
- Our conduct must be without _____ .
- We must be strong and of good courage.

The Promise:
- The Lord is our helper. And He is always with us.

There are two ways to use God's promises:
- To stand on the promises in your test of faith.
- To reach out in hope and hold on to the promises in order to do great things for God.

Group Discussion

Take a few moments to consider these questions, then discuss.

What promise do you need to claim right now?

_____

_____

Do you find it difficult to praise and worship the Lord for your problems? _____

_____

From experience what happens if you praise and worship the Lord? _____

_____

On a Personal Level

	Never	Occasionally	Often
To suffer for the Lord gives me joy.	O	O	O
It is easy to conquer little faith.	O	O	O
During a test I always ask the Lord to show me my unbelief.	O	O	O
I praise God during tests.	O	O	O
Covetousness is not a part of my behavior.	O	O	O

Self Assessment
Are you claiming the promises of God?

THE
TESTING
OF YOUR
FAITH

The Character of God

"And the LORD passed before him and
proclaimed, 'The LORD, the LORD God,
merciful and gracious, long-suffering, and
abounding in goodness and truth."
Exodus 34:6

We Must Know Our Tester!

- When someone causes you a lot of pain there is usually a breach of trust.
- We are in tests that are from God above. When we endure the test we become stronger.
- If you fail you will become angry at God.
- We must know the characteristics of God, our tester.

5 Characteristics of God

Exodus 34:5-6—"Then the LORD descended in the cloud and stood with him there, and proclaimed the name of the LORD. And the LORD passed before him and proclaimed, 'The LORD, the LORD God, merciful and gracious, long-suffering, and abounding in goodness and truth."

1. God is _____ .

- The word means the same as a mother's womb.
- The most intimate relationship.
- Overwhelming compassion.

2. God is _____ .

- To have pity.
- To give freely something undeserved.

3. God is _____ .

• To keep His anger for a long time.

4. God is abounding in _____ .

• His lovingkindness.
• God is overwhelmingly loyal.

5. God is abounding in _____ .

• God is faithful.
• He is our security.
• He is truth.

Ask God for His Lovingkindness

In a test of faith, if you ask God for His lovingkindness.
He will always extend it to you, because God is merciful,
gracious, long-suffering, abounding in goodness and in
truth.

Group Discussion

Take a few moments to consider these questions, then discuss.

What would you consider the main characteristics of God?

_____

_____

Share with the group a characteristic of God that is at present the most precious to you. _____

_____

On a Personal Level

When I am in a test I always believe:	Never	Occasionally	Often
God cares for me.	◯	◯	◯
God has unlimited mercy.	◯	◯	◯
God is long-suffering. He won't punish immediately.	◯	◯	◯
God is loyal.	◯	◯	◯
God's Word is the truth.	◯	◯	◯

Self Assessment
Is your belief about God's character lacking, growing or strong?

THE
TESTING
OF YOUR
FAITH

Seeking God's Wisdom

"If any of you lacks wisdom, let him ask of God,
who gives to all liberally and without reproach,
and it will be given to him."
James 1:5

SESSION TWELVE

When You Don't Know What to Do

James 1:2-8—"My brethren, count it all joy when you fall into various trials, knowing that the testing of your faith produces patience. But let patience have its perfect work, that you may be perfect and complete, lacking nothing. If any of you lacks wisdom, let him ask of God, who gives to all liberally and without reproach, and it will be given to him. But let him ask in faith, with no doubting, for he who doubts is like a wave of the sea driven and tossed by the wind. For let not that man suppose that he will receive anything from the LORD; He is a double-minded man, unstable in all his ways."

- "If any of you lacks wisdom"
  The Condition

- "Let him ask of God"
  The Command

- "Who gives to all liberally"
  The Promise

- "Without reproach"
  The Promise

- "And it will be given to him"
  The Promise

- "But let him ask in faith"
  The Command

- "With no doubting"
  The Command

- "For he who doubts is like a wave of the sea driven and tossed by the wind"
  The Outcome

- "For let not that man suppose that he will receive anything from the Lord"
  The Outcome

- "He is a double-minded man"

- "Unstable in all his ways"

- The purpose of testing is for our _____

- The purpose of temptation is for our _____

1 Corinthians 10:13—"No temptation has overtaken you except as is common to man; but God is faithful, who will not allow you to be tempted beyond that which you are able, but with the temptation will also make the way of escape, that you may be able to bear it."

- God will never allow you to be tempted beyond that which you are able to endure. He will give you a way out.

Group Discussion

Take a few moments to consider these questions, then discuss.

What did you learn about God's wisdom in this session?

_____

_____

Discuss the difference between a test and a temptation.

_____

_____

What did this series do to your faith?

_____

_____

On a Personal Level

Which test did you try to escape from? _____

_____

In previous tests did you say, "I don't know the answer?"

_____

Have you asked God for the answer to your tests?

_____

What is your reaction if God doesn't answer your prayers directly?

_____

Did God recently ask you to do something which you refused?

_____

Leader's Notes and Answer Key

Welcome to *The Testing of Your Faith!*

Plan Your Time

Each video session is approximately 28 minutes in length.

If you are viewing this series in a small group setting, it is suggested that you provide 45 minutes for discussion following the video viewing of each session. Discussion questions are provided in the workbook at the end of each session.

Answer Key

Session One
mature, complete, lacking.
1. the faith of every
- little while
- need
- pain
- various
- genuine faith
- precious
- faith
2. everything
3. every
4. control
5. unlimited

Session Two
6. pass
7. good

Session Three
- faithful
- unfaithful
Five Wrong Responses:
1. compromise
2. complain
3. criticize
4. against, anger
5. corrupt, faith

Session Four
1. teaches
everything
covenant
2. response
complain and murmur
3. chastens
bless

Session Five
1. grief
- emotionally
3. act
4. feeling
5. wrong

Session Six
- faith
- past
- glory

Session Seven
- hope
- forget
- commandments
- memories
- promises
- promises, faith
- faith
- **Past-** 17
- **Future –** 17

Session Eight
- daily
2. Record
3. 10
4. Retrace
5. memorials

Session Nine
(no fill-ins)

Session Ten
- reward
- requests
- peace
- Confess
- Serve
- not trusting God
- covetousness

Session Eleven
1. merciful
2. gracious
3. long-suffering
4. goodness
5. truth

Session Twelve
- good
- harm

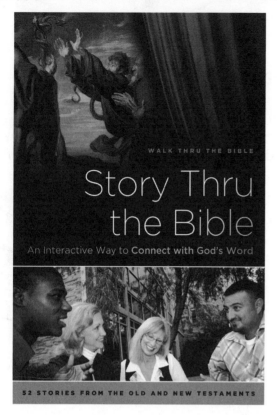

52 Interactive Bible Stories for all ages

Engage in God's Story— in a whole new way!

Storying through the Bible is an engaging, highly effective, and natural way to communicate key truths, concepts, and values of God's Word, and to pass it on to others.

Story Thru the Bible helps people tell the major stories of the Bible effectively and faithfully with minimal study and preparation. Anyone can lead or participate in storying—even if they have no previous knowledge of the Bible!

Ideal for small groups and families or for personal reading and growth.

Each story includes a summary, engaging questions, and practical ways you and your listeners can apply what has been learned.

Story Thru the Bible. It's God's story. It's your story.
Listen. Share. Grow.

336 Pages, Paperback
www.storythruthebible.org
1.800.361.6131